TAKE FIVE 05

TAKE FIVE 05

CATHERINE BYRON
JOHN LUCAS
CLARE MACDONALD SHAW
PETER PORTER
GREGORY WOODS

All rights reserved. No part of this work covered by the copyright hereon may be reproduced or used in any form by any means – graphic, electronic, or mechanical, including copying, recording, taping, or information storage and retrieval systems – without written permission of the publisher.

Typeset and Printed by Q3 Print Project Management Ltd,
Loughborough, Leics
(01509) 213456

Published by Shoestring Press
19 Devonshire Avenue, Beeston, Nottingham, NG9 1BS
Telephone: (0115) 925 1827
www.shoestringpress.co.uk

First published 2005
© Copyright: Catherine Byron, John Lucas, Clare MacDonald Shaw, Peter Porter and Gregory Woods

ISBN: 1 904886 17 5

Contents

CATHERINE BYRON
The Winter Husband — 3

JOHN LUCAS
The Night we Called it a Day — 15

CLARE MacDONALD SHAW
Post-Mortem — 27

PETER PORTER
At the Botanical Gardens, Rome — 41
Whereof We Cannot Speak — 44
The Thirty-nine Articles — 45
Is this a Political Sonnet? Tick the Appropriate Box — 46
The Judgment of Cambyses — 47
Improvisation A.M. — 48
Up Close — 49
George Crabbe at "The White Hart" — 50
At the Reunion of the Answers — 51
Riding with Dante — 52

GREGORY WOODS
Sir Osbert's Complaint — 57

For Dick Ellis

Catherine Byron

Catherine Byron grew up in Belfast, raised daughters and goats in the West of Scotland, and now lives in the English Midlands, where she teaches writing and medieval literature at Nottingham Trent University. Her first collection (*Settlements*, 1985) was hailed as a 'classic of Irish exile': it has been reprinted several times. In 1992 she published *Out of Step: Pursuing Seamus to Purgatory*, an avowedly personal reading of Heaney's 'Station Island' sequence. Her most recent collection, *The Getting of Vellum* (Salmon, 2000), was inspired by her ongoing creative collaboration with Dublin-based artist/calliographer Denis Brown.

Byron writes for the page, the voice and the web. She is currently poet in residence at Sunderland University's International Institute of Glass, in creative conversation with several artists working in glass that is at the heart of her three year AHRC Creative Fellowship in Writing. The over-arching theme of her Fellowship project is a series of poetic re-imaginings of Chaucer's gappy, draughty, wickerwork Hous of Rumour, the final *locus* in his incomplete dream-vision poem *Hous of Fame*. *The Winter Husband* is one fruit of this re-imagining.

Acknowledgements:

An earlier version of 'Epithalamion for Midsummer Day' was published in *The Fat-Hen Field Hospital* (Byron, 1993). Earlier versions of two sections of 'The Winter Husband' appear in *The Getting of Vellum* (Byron, 2000) as part of the volume's dedicatory poem, and as 'The Hotel Hades'. The 'January's gone' section is adapted from the sound script of the new media work *Creel of Voices* which was first performed at the 'Writers of the Future Roadshow', Midlands Arts Centre, Birmingham, on 22 June 2004. Byron is a member of the TEXTLAB group of writers brought together for the NESTA funded 'Writers of the Future' project (2003–2005) by the trAce Online Writing Community at Nottingham Trent University.

The penultimate section of 'The Winter Husband' is a version of 'Thoughts in the Quiet Night' by Li P'o (701–762).

Patrick Leigh Fermor's *Mani: Travels in the Southern Peloponnese* was first published in 1958 by John Murray.

Catherine Byron is grateful to the Arts & Humanities Research Council for a three year Creative Fellowship in Writing 2003 – 2006, and for technical and creative support from the trAce Online Writing Centre.

THE WINTER HUSBAND

> *Any marriage, happy or unhappy,*
> *is more interesting than a love-affair.*
> W H Auden in a letter to Thekla Clarke

I

Epithalamion for Midsummer Day
  in the Glens of Antrim

Last night the bonefires spoke
to the sun, calling its gold
down onto corn set green.

Today there has been no let
to the rain that spills and rivers
staining the ash with dark.

By evening there'll be a gush
will build its humming spate
to a force, a waterfall

and we'll roll our pleasures down
the tumble of filmy hills
in the long midsummer dusk.

Tonight on our first hearth
I will smoor the fire
this night and every night
each single night

II

The Winter Husband

O Sisters from Tyrone and
  West Belfast

who schooled us in the
  custody of the eyes

and how a girl must always
  close her legs

and keep a watch for Satan
  on the bus –

those cloven hooves
  a giveaway under suits –

is your *hors de combat*
  wisdom any use

to a woman who chose marriage,
  and still burns?

A girl in the thick of it,
  but getting none?

   ★

I'm lying in bed dreaming a corpse beside me.
Yes, he's died in the night, and that's him gone and cold
and an end of all that thwarting. No more NOs.

I'm well shot of him, though I know it is
a terrible thing to be lying beside him dead
while the other one, my husband, where is he?

    The winter man and I
    slur out of sleep
    avoiding touch. Our
    separate fleshes creep.

O sisters mine, I think it may be – possession.

    *

There's a devil in my man.
    It makes him lie
on the bridge parapet.
    He plans to die.

When a train rattles under
    he'll simply roll
off, and that devil
    will catch his soul.

O my sisters
    how'll I cast
this devil out?
    He cannot last,

this changeling man,
    but if he dies
in his winter skin
    will my real man die?

    *

Where are you, man of summer,
midsummer man I married?
I expect that changeling now
as light drains fast through September.

I'm getting to know the signs
of impending substitution.
You fade from under your skin,
your irises cloud with absence.

By Michaelmas you are gone.
The winter husband is here
and there's no shifting him until
the equinox at the other

chilly end of winter.

    ★

January's gone
  and the year's
    tilting away from night
      the star-bowl's shifting

A settling now
  the drift
    centred and soft

Weight
  with the pull of light
    against dark
      done with

    ★

Come Easter I'll be making
my way to the handover place.
I'll take this winter man
and dump him. Run to meet

you coming. Every spring
you're slower, though, more sealed.
You trail the hostage-slime
of time in solitary.

Each year more frost on you.
Each summer's further north.
Our bedsheets stiffen.
We are each alone.

> *God love ye, girl, there's not much comfort there.*
> *For pity's sake, would ye not turn to Jesus?*

I went alone to Kilclooney,
St Mary's church at the crossroads.
The host like a great slow snowflake
fizzled on my warm wet tongue
as brief and come-and-gone sweet
as candyfloss, and that
is the closest I got to having
sex with a man this Easter,
this whole winter.
     Jesus?
O sisters, in your dreams.

> *Deario, and Him the best of lovers!*
> *Still and all, ye chose a mortal man.*

> *If he's a prisoner held against his will*
> *ye'll simply have to go to hell to fetch him.*

> *There's surely many a plot to guide ye down,*
> *and many a clue to help youse out together.*

My celibate sisters, you gave me
an excellent grounding in gods.
Like all your maps for living
the root directory's *Rome*:
the soft Italiany *ch*'s
of the old Tridentine Mass,
but you also coached us in
the harder *k*'s of its other
pagan tongues. Classic:

Carmina, Metamorphoses,
seminal texts on sex.
And death. And hell. A truly
catholic vision of the world.

So I'll try the pagan routes
you schooled me in on rainy
Belfast afternoons
under the Black Mountain
and on the nod.

⭐

GO to Aeneas' quest in the souterrain of Pluto.

> Avernus, the birdless lake?
> the easiest descent,
> the toughest to retrace?
> Aeneas made it, but
> brought no-one back.

GO to Odysseus, then, yon wily fixer.

> Dodona, is it? There
> he poured fresh blood in a trench
> and then cold fluids such
> as we the living swallow –
> honey and milk, sweet wine,
> and finally spring water.
> He scattered white barley grains
> over the puddled earth
> and began to talk with the dead –
> the senseless, feeble dead.

But he brought no-one back.

GO to Orpheus –

    The nearly nearly man?

Well, don't GO to Alcestis, the wife who died instead!

    Even Demeter, sisters,
    even the god Demeter
    could only win her Persephone
    back for half the year.

Wasn't there one smart girl who pulled it off
whose very name means Soul?

    Wait till I tell you, sisters,
    I got there just before you!
    I'm thinking another entrance,
    and another text altogether,
    the book I read and reread
    in chilly Belfast weathers
    dreaming the Greece of now.

    I have it still, in its jacket
    of bleached-out yellow and blue,
    the hand-drawn letters: *Mani* –
    my better-than-bible, my inkling
    in Belfast days that another
    land than Mother Ireland
    might be my holy ground.

    Way back then I promised
    my self I'd one day sail
    to the farthest southern tip
    of three-fingered Peloponnísos,
    that *last sharp edge of rock*
    Patrick Leigh Fermor grasped
    when his caïque's engine spluttered
    rounding Cape Taínaron:

this quick, rough contact with
the mark his finger 'd *often*
covered on the atlas page –
I loved and learnt from his
metamorphosis of touch:
from page to rock, and then
his plunge from page into sea.

Is now the time I dreamed of?
Can I sail with winter man
to Taínaros' sea-drowned cave
and swim in its waters, like Fermor?
The men of Yerolimín
say it's the vent into Hades
that Psyche clambered through
to run downhill to Eros.

Sisters, you have her right:
the Soul searching for Eros.
But is Eros Love? or Desire?

★

No matter, girl. Just GO there with our blessing
and celebrate Greek Easter with your man.
The way their calendar falls this year, you've got
another week before the new fire's kindled
and eggs are cracked, and 'Christos anesté' sung.

★

I've booked us a budget flight
me and the winter husband

from Aldergrove's icy runways
straight into Máni's spring.

I feel his winter breath
on my neck at embarkation.

I watch its frost recoil
as we step through the oval door

of the plane at Kalamáta.
Dark tarmac. Glassy heat.

Not spring, but sudden summer
takes his breath away.

On the bus-ride into town
he turns his face from the sun.

       ★

    I thought to hasten summer
    but found I was there alone

    after one last going-down
    in our bed at Hotel Hades:

In the old town, a shuttered afternoon.
The black redstart, lover of broken ground
warbles its song, a grinding of metal on metal,
a 'tsip tucc-tucc', and then its song again.
In the old hotel, shuttered siesta time.
Your cock rises again from its dark wood.
I take upon my tongue the dew of cum
that's beading on your glans. My every mouth
is famine-hungry for you. I don't ask
if, where you've been, you sucked the cock of Hades.
Does semen count as seed? Like pomegranate's?

    ★

Sisters, I remember what you said:
that when a human's ready to let go
of mortal life, there'll often be a brief
and lovely mini-summer, just a day
perhaps, when she or he is back within
their heart and hand and head, and best of all
back, beyond all hope, for one last spell
fully within their skin. Radiant. There.

And though you often blushed to talk of sex
you taught us girls a most important fact:
that skin's the largest organ humans have,
and that it speaks our deepest, dearest selves
unto the hearing, listening skin of another.
I thank you for these lessons long ago.

In his short summer lease before we part
I lean and listen, in my love and grief
and lay my skin against his suddenly-
bright-with-presence skin, and hear the last
skinwhispers of our old commingling selves.
I feel his skin grow dim, and quieten.

   ★

In the small hours
I woke alone
to moonlight.

For a moment
I thought it was frost
on the cool floor.

When I lifted my head
I saw it at once –
the moon.

I bowed my head
and thought of
my distant home.

   ★

At dawn I rose with the sun
and walked down through

the olive groves to
Kalamáta's sea.

John Lucas

John Lucas is Professor Emeritus of the Universities of Loughborough and Nottingham Trent. As well as being the author of numerous books of a critical and scholarly nature, he has published seven collections of poetry, including *Studying Grosz the Bus* (winner of the 1990 Aldeburgh Poetry Prize), *A World Perhaps: New & Selected Poems* (2002) and *The Long and the Short of It* (2004). In 1994 he began Shoestring Press.

THE NIGHT WE CALLED IT A DAY

It was Doug's new wheeze and, as he ran the band,
    we said "yes, boss", though we weren't that thrilled.
"She looks good, sings great, she'll bring the punters back,
    and bums on seats means cash in the till,
put a smile on the landlord's cheesy old face.
    Lads, we need this, or it's face the sack."

Scare tactics. Doug gets these urges. So: bowlers,
    bow-ties, kilts – we've done the lot. "The Biz"
he calls it, "Keeping the Image Fresh." I wish!
    Same semi-pros. equals the same score:
Muskrat, Basin Street, Snag It, and of course Doug's
    feature. Guess what? *Stranger on the Shore.*

He called a practice. This was now serious.
    Pete came straight from his shop, blew some notes,
asked, "what do you reckon?" "Well, Louis it's not …"
    Simon bent over his strings, sump-oiled
nails spanning the frets. "About this new bird, dad."
    "New? You jest. All Doug's goods are shop-soiled."

Dave set up snare and hi-hat. "I passed your van
    this a.m." Don said, greasing his slide,
"Down Bulwell." "Gas leak." "*Really? And* yesterday?"
    "You running gumshoe?" "Just this week's round –
parcels. You're quiet, Kenneth. School still standing?"
    "Fine" I said. "Has someone got an A?"

And then Doug arrived and we all stood, eyes front,
    watched him lead her up. She was slim, tall,
suede jacket, cotton top, tight black jeans, high heels,
    and he was the cat who's got the cream.
"This, lads, is Chloe with the golden tonsils,
    come to help us realise our dream."

"What's that when it's at home?" "Numero Uno
   Midlands Band you berk, Pete," Doug ground out,
"like we once was." "A bit before my time then."
   "True, Donald," Doug said, "so let's all hope
you're still with us when the good times roll again."
   Nasty Doug could be, when he'd the scope.

"Right", he rapped. "*Georgia*. From the top. Key of F."
   "I sing it in G." Like a stuffed cod
he gawped at her. "G? ...**G???** ... Simon, we got that?"
   "With verse", she added. The cod blinked. "Verse?
Right. *Right*." We busked it through and at the end she
   grimaced. "Well, it can't get any worse."

"Don't speak too soon" Don warned, as Doug flicked over
   his hit list, suggested *Sister Kate*.
"I'd sooner die", she groaned. "Try *Weeping Willow*."
   "It's in the book." Simon plunked some chords,
we joined him and now the band started to cruise
   among the sharp reefs of Bessie's words

while Chloe's voice steered us home. On the last note
   I winked at Pete, who looked at Doug who
stood, eyes closed, tasting double cream and grinning
   before he asked her "Got any more
where that came from?" Had she? *Lover Man, Pennies,
   Darn that Dream, Sugar*. Then, an unsure

moment. Calm as paint she said, "I'll sing *Strange Fruit*
   to end with, and bass backing alone."
"Great" I said, and the others all said "Great", bar
   Doug, who couldn't do sincere. "A shade
downbeat for a closer. I had in mind *A
   Porter's Lovesong to a Chambermaid*.

That's a swinger." "You're all taste, Doug," she laughed and
    he reddened. No contest. Still, he had
to show who was in charge. "I've been thinking you'll
    need a change of name. Something to fix
in Joe Public's mind. Bluesy but sweet, something
    to look good with "DOUG DANVILLE'S HOT SIX."

(Fanatics have their dreams.) "Billie?" "Patented"
    Doug told Dave, "Still B's right, B for Blues,
what d'you call words that start with the same letter?"
    "Electrification?" "Sod off, Pete."
"Belle?" Don offered. "Belle." Doug tried it. "Belle – yeh, ace.
    Suit you, love?" Chloe studied her feet

then, "Whatever." But she gave him a big smile
    so cream was now back on the menu.
"Right, we'll go with Belle. And lads, scruff order's out,
    white shirts, black trousers, ties, keep it smart.
I'll get some posters done, phone Al at the *NEWS*:
    next session we'll blow the place apart.

Till Friday, then!" "Wait. One more thing." Chloe's long
    crimson-lake nails gleamed in the spotlight.
"I'll sing eight numbers toto. The middle set."
    Rancid cream! He said, "I'd hoped we might
spread the songs round all the sets." "What, on the dosh
    you pay? No chance. One set and Goodnight.

See you boys." And she was gone. "Give her a month",
    Doug tried his smirk, "she'll fall into line."
"If she lasts that long," Dave said. "She's a Big Time
    Gal. Needs an agent though." "She's got me."
"*You?*" Smirk, smirk. "I'd call this a good career move.
    For us all of course. Bring on Friday!"

The bar was filling when I lugged my bass through:
    we'd got used to forty max. but now
60 at least were in with more arriving.
        Old faces, names, the HOTSHOTS, half TURK'S
            JAZZMEN,
greetings, handshakes, and banter. "You still blowing?"
    "While the teeth last. What's with tonight, then?"

"You'll see." Doug had done his work well. By the first
    break the place was heaving. But – Problem!
No Chloe. "She'll be here", but Doug was looking
    like he'd swallowed puke. Then suddenly
"Hi. boys", and here she was. Wow. Page-boy, halter-
    top black number. Doug got a friendly

peck as she winked at us. "Ready when you are."
    We took the drinks on stage, went into
Weeping Willow Blues and her voice knocked them flat.
    Encore for that, for each song encore,
and after *Strange Fruit* (the landlord dimmed the lights)
    dead silence and then – solid uproar.

Follow that! Fat hope. The last set plunged downhill
    though the band was high and Dave on traps
became the city's answer to George Whetling.
    But the crowd had got all they'd paid for
and left before the end. While we packed up, Dave
    grumbled, "so now she'll be our saviour."

"Too right!" "What's she get then, Doug?" "Same as us all."
    "*Thirty?*" "Plus her full share of the pot."
"She'll want more than that." "She's on the bottom rung,
    learning her trade, like *we had to*."
"Seems to me she's learnt it." I watched Doug redden.
    "That's for me to decide, Pete, not *you*."

Take that! "Right lads. Same time next week." Come next week
    it was gravy time. Full House and Belle
was stellar: same set, same order, but her voice
    came fuller, richer. "Like crushed velvet"
Don opined when we were divvying the pot.
    Doug was blithe. "You ain't heard nothing yet."

Next week, she dropped in a tribute to the Duke:
Don't Get Around Much, then *Satin Doll*.
Simon on guitar plucked chords from out the deep
    and when we finished the joint went wild.
One Hooray was pleading to buy her drinks but
    she shook him off, blew us kisses, smiled

nighty-night and went. As per, the final set
    was flatter than last night's beer. The crowd
thinned to the geriatric faithful and though
    we tried, its hard blowing when you know
no punter's come to hear *you*. As my old mum
    would say "After the Lord Mayor's Show …"

"How about Belle's taking the last set?" Don risked,
    as we stowed our gear. "At least that way
the crowd might stay to the end. And where the hell
    is she off to when she leaves here?" "Home."
Doug was terse. "She's a serious one. But, yes,
    Don, we'll go with TOP OF THE BILL BELLE."

More posters. Next week was chocka. Nobody
    left and *Strange Fruit* got three whole encores.
Belle deserved the cheers, and the band was lifted.
    But all things end. Up came the houselights
and "If you want more come earlier next time"
    Doug called. He was flying – on the heights,

Stout Cortez of the clarinet. Still, something
    bugged me. Not with Belle's work, nor the band's –
We were a tight outfit now. But at the bar
    I'd seen what I hadn't liked. A Skin:
sagged jeans, ferkin belly, and on his T shirt
    A message DONT LET THE BUGGERS WIN.

Playing bass, you can see what others miss – Dave
    dreaming he's down in Crescent City,
Si's gaze clamped on the chords, Pete's eyes shut so's not
    to meet the pain on a punter's face
(ho, ho). The Skin had left early, and when I
    told them, Doug said, "he felt out of place,

perhaps." "Pull the other one." Don, who's ex-plod
    looked stern. "Form says he'll be back next week,
with some of his mates in tow." Spot on. Next time
    ten brickhouse uglies stood at the bar
lagered up, and waiting for Belle's set to start.
    She'd just hit stride when a banana

smacked down at her feet. Another, followed by
    "Who let the coon in?" "Keep Britain white".
"Get back to the jungle, coon, cunt, black bastard."
    A slow handclap, thud of bovver boots,
and now they linked arms in front of the bandstand,
    skull swastikas and Hitler salutes.

"You comin' down or d'we climb up to get you?"
    last week's hero enquired. "You fat pig",
Belle spat. "You ugly moron, I bet your prick's
    this long", crooking her little finger.
He blinked as a few of them sniggered. Then red-
    eyed he turned on them. "Shut it. Bring her

down here," hand on studded belt. "If I were you
 I'd watch out for my back", Don warned him.
Next moment the Boys in Blue came hurtling through
 front and side doors. BANG. Punters scattered
as, hand-cuffed, harmless, the Skins were herded out –
 a table went, some glasses shattered,

but it was all done and dusted in a trice,
 normal service resumed. We finished
the set and then, with Belle silent, talked it through.
 Don had tipped off the Bill. "A good thing"
the landlord sniffed, when he paid Doug. "Right bastards,
 if I had my way I'd see them swing.

They'll get this place a bad name. You ok, love,
 you had to take a lot, you looked scared
to buggery." She shrugged. "You get used to it."
 But her voice was flat and I could tell
she was biting back the tears. We all nodded
 when Simon said, "may they rot in hell."

So, crisis averted? Yes and no. Next night
 local TV featured a piece on
TOP CITY PUB TARGETTED BY RACIST THUGS
 with Doug blowing some notes. "Leader well
dischuffed but the band played on." Then the city
 rag had as Monday's headline *BELLE'S HELL.*

But that was nothing compared to the next gig.
 BBC and ITV sent crews,
there were hacks, snappers, "Look this way, please, darlin'"
 as Belle entered (earlier this time)
drinks for us all, landlord in his one good suit,
 and, by arrangement, Belle sang *Strange Fruit*

first up so the London crowd could file copy
        for next morning's redtops. Once they'd gone
the show went down like a pint of mucus. Not
        even Belle could lift us and our mood
got to the crowd. Soon they were leaving in droves
        as though rumours had spread – "for a good

time try some other place." But Doug was upbeat:
        "Don't fret, lads, we're onto something big."
He was, he meant. Next gig, neither Belle, nor Doug,
        (*and* he put a naff dep. in on reeds.)
"They're down the Smoke", Pete said. "Frith Street called and now
        the Park wants her. Seems the whole world needs

our Blues Belle, with Mr 10 Per Cent close by
        to guide her progress – and grease his palm!"
There were few in next Friday, fewer the next.
        The one after that we made our last.
No Belle, no Doug, no crowd, and no one wanted
        to lead the band. "That's it, we're the past,

last week's news", Simon mourned. "We've had ten good years"
        Pete consoled him. "Tell me how many
bands can claim that much?" The landlord shook hands, pushed
        drinks across the bar. "All on the house."
We drank a toast to the music. "What's to come
        after us?" Dave asked him. "I'm not rushed,

but Country & Western brings them in elsewhere."
        Two weeks later I saw in the *NEWS*
an Ad; *"CINDY AND HER FELLERS AT THE STAG
        THIS FRIDAY NIGHT!!!"* He'd not wasted time.
Six months later *KARAOKE* filled the bill.
        By then Belle was hot news, seemed to climb

another rung each week. Tour, T.V., film – she
       played night-club singer in the re-make
of a gangster *Noire* who marries Mister Big.
       Which reminds me – our one time leader,
Doug, was bought out by a Mega Agency.
       Dave brought us all the news one night when we

five met for a drink. "Lads, have you ever thought
       that punch-up could have been Doug's last wheeze?"
Si. asked. "To get Belle on the front page. I mean
       how did they all *know*? Unless your bright
lads slipped it to Fleet Street's finest?" "No," Don said:
       "Dirty Doug laid all the plans that night."

"You reckon?" Don tapped his nose. "Once a copper ..."
       It made sense. Doug was a fixer. We've
caught the odd glimpse of him since, blonde on arm, or
       smug behind the wheel of some flash car.
"Doug Ace-in-the-Hole" we call him. As for Belle,
       she's into orbit now. Belle's a Star.

Clare MacDonald Shaw

Clare MacDonald Shaw, raised in Herefordshire and South London, now lives in Nottingham. She read English at Oxford and taught in London and America. For several years she edited the poetry magazine *Quartz*. At Nottingham Trent University she lectures in Modernism and Women's Writing 1780–1865, and has also taught Romanticism and the poetry option on the M.A. in Creative Writing. She has published research articles and an edition of Hannah More's *Tales for the Common People* in 2002.

Her poems have appeared in various journals and anthologies including *The Independent, Times Literary Supplement, London Magazine, Poetry Wales, The Poetry Book Society Anthology 1992, The Observer Arvon Poetry Collection 1993, The TLS/Poems on the Underground Prizewinners' Booklet 1996,* and *The Bridport Prize Anthology 1997.* A chapbook – *How Ghosts Begin* – was published by Shoestring Press in 1997; her first full collection, *Blue Fever*, came from Blackwater Press, 1999.

POST-MORTEM

Abbess Hildegard of Bingen, visionary writer and preacher, was called 'old Scrumpilgard' by a wicked spirit in a woman's body.

1. Child Burial

*Ash of ash,
rot of corruption,
say and write
what you hear and see.*

Her Latin fogs my brain,
and she's dust of dust,
Sounds humble enough,
but that black cloth *Life*
suggests a will to power:
I find her *Works*, and
Vita Sanctae Hildegardis
by Godfrey and Theodoric,
shelf-bound with the patriarchs.

Fierce and wily abbess,
maker of passionate songs,
she-preacher, shut up now
in a theology book-stack,
Hildegard once had bishops,
popes and kings by the nose.

In her eighth year, 1106,
this tenth child, given to God
was enclosed in a cell, buried
by priests and parents.
Torches, words, darkness.
Funeral rites for Hildegard,
walled up for life with Jutta,
anchoress. They read psalters,
kept the vigils of God, matins
to cold first light.

How to survive? A window but
no door; servants to pass beer,
beans and waste through the hole.
Plainchant from a monastery
above, protecting and inspecting.
She stitched in gold, perhaps, or
mended vestments for priests.
Others came to catch their holiness.
Cell grew to convent; new vows
for the enclosed. That should
have been all, but in middle age,
at a stroke, she was transfixed:

in the year 1141,
when I was forty-two years
and seven months old,
a fiery blinding light
from the opening of heaven
poured through my whole brain.

Life began; visions gave her power,
which grew. Celestial adviser
to the great, prophetic diplomat,
she wrote to queens and kings,
practised arts and sciences.
When this life palled –
born a third time perhaps
at sixty – she broke enclosure,
went preaching round villages.

2. Gothic Voices

Her music's been released.
Light plays on silver,
but the text is locked:

    O Ecclesia,
oculi tui similes saphyro sunt

what are these sapphire eyes
of the Church? To us no more
than painted windows.

Ursula loved the son of God:
  in multo desiderio
I have desired to come to you.

In honour of St Ursula,
who gave up earthly marriage,
these glass voices
pierce and splinter cells,
Air stabbed by laser
makes octave leaps,
too sudden for hymns.
A stone mouth might sing
this high radar to vaults
after the great door slams,
icy hinge between worlds.

3. Blindsight

The CD's jewel-box
hoards a manuscript; did she
leaf gold, grind lapis herself
or dictate paint to a monk?
Her God's a bull's eye,
coiled fire rolling
over scorched earth.
Stars burn out, whizz
down to her page:

signs of migraine, according
to scholars: specks on the retina,
twelfth-century blues.
We'd cure defective vision –
far sight, auras, floaters,
the saint's *astigmata*,
her fiery blinding.

What has she put down?
That she sees at all times
a shadow of the living light,
umbra viventis luminis;
rarely, the light itself.

4. Transmitter

Be more explicit, please,
for modern sceptics.
She sounds tough-minded,
might have something to report.
Those back from the core of dark
want news of other journeys.

I look up scholars
and spell out her Latin, but
she's alien beyond recall.
The voice is clear, insistent,
questions stabbing text:
Quis? Quae? Quomodo?
Receiver and transmitter,
diviner, spout of God,
her politics were authorized.
Decodings undertaken,
warnings given
to all the courts of Europe.

Such women's speech
had licence (sound booms
from empty vessels) but
she made sure to call herself
miserrima, unvoicing pride,
although she ran two convents.
The sisters acted out her dialogues –
Lucifer takes on Chastity; she wins,
transcending nature. Rumour said
that high-born nuns dressed up
in diadems to sing her sequences:
Ave, generosa.

5. Science for Women

She wrote science. *Physica* lists
properties of stones: carbuncles grow
in the moon's eclipse; amethyst is good
for spots on your face, and for some pains
I can't translate it looks as if
a topaz in the rectum helps.

I'm losing faith in this.
The birds, though, sound real:
De Ulula, De Cuculo:
About the Owl and Cuckoo,
croaking local *Kraha* too;
but the *Widehoppo?*
Could you spot it from a cell?

We have views on authority;
how could she be sure
parrots were of no use
in medicine? Compiled, we'd say
from doubtful sources,

Her *Causes and Cures*,
analysing women's health,
is more convincing; aloe and myrrh
for headaches or *emigranea*.
For years she's treated souls
enclosed against their flesh;

knows melancholics,
disliked by men for coldness.
Erotic joy, if any, quickly
fades for them; they suffer
swelling legs and backache,
go mad untreated.

Like one these women,
Stoneheart takes shape
in the *Book of Life's Merits* –
a writer's other self –
who gathers like bitter smoke,
dark as the core of vision.
Sullen, indifferent, she says,
more formally than this:

I have made nothing,
brought no one to life.
Why should I give a damn?
All I know is that I am.

Mercy reproves her: flowers
give off scent, gems don't hoard
their sparkle, but she's a stone,
a cold eye, staring.

Another vision.
Sadness waiting under a tree;
it has dried up, leaves gone,
ungreen. A branch is reaching
out for her. Green's *viriditas*,
pagan sap redeemed.

Soul is to body
as sap is to tree.

The spirit green
igniting fields
joins the spectral play
of water, moon and star
in their perpetual
spontaneous combustion.

6. Cryptics

But modern sight
misreads her images. Look,
a young nun: fire shooting up
from her eyes, or holy tongues
of flame descending? She holds
wax tablets; a monk observes.

Even if I stood near enough
to see what's written, I'd be
none the wiser. She invented
a lost *écriture* for women,
tongue and word and cipher

Lingua ignota, litterae ignotae;

female mystery, and useful code
to fend off prying eyes of priests,
before she led the nuns
in exodus to genesis,
dragged them out of Egypt
to a muddy building site.
Monks lost rich dowries;
she sold plots of holy ground
on the new land for burials.
With cash, stones and mortar,
woman's rule began.

When clerics thwarted her
she took to bed and sickened
till the fools gave in. Prophets
had to be heard: divine will
took them over, ventriloquizing
through the puppet. Direct access
to God's mind was her insurance,
though the cost came high; visions
filled and drained her.

　　　　　　And questioners
began to check her sources; the devil
might have wormed her, bred
delusions. For a saintly referee,
she tried Bernard of Clairvaux,
wrote him a diplomatic letter.
Two years back she'd seen him
in a vision, eagle above men,
looking bravely into the sun.
This seemed to him a truthful insight,
Wisdom being a great bird.

7. Uncanonical

He's safely canonized
in history; why did it hold
no trace of her in schoolbooks
totting up popes or anti-popes
she might have known? After death
she went unsainted. Was there
more strength than virtue in her,
did she draw more fear than love?

Or did men quietly reset
the scales of power
when that alarming voice
cut out, when the ghosted breath
had gone, when she no longer
blackmailed souls with threats
of being erased for ever
from the Book of Life
for interfering with her words
like this?

Something unsaintly here –
fierce imagination, force of will.
What she calls vision
in a secular age
is read as art: figures
move on the inner shell
of the skull, expressionist
in colour; brilliant,
her use of aura.

Others go beyond;
we're eager to reclaim her.
Critics analyse and praise
unconscious energies
and semiotic flux.
Yet she worships
a symbolic order, gives
no dispensations to her sex,
lets no rival share her power.

It went out with her, firework,
dried stick falling to earth,
consuming her in a glorious blaze
which lit up life a moment.
So we translate her into
our time. What did status
of weak clay count
for a chosen spirit
circling the sun?

8. Scrumpilgard

As flesh and blood,
how did she run a convent:
singing school, or prison of the heart?
To the young nun Richardis –
secretary, friend, disciple –
she was still a matriarch.
For years Richardis read,
took dictation, waited.
Bolted for promotion
far off in the north.

Hildegard writes to her:
she has been abandoned;
her sorrow calls
to all who suffer like her,
who mourn life torn away.
Tries the black art of rhetoric
against her; asks the pope
to intervene. Such traitors
soon fall sick, and die.

Years later, there was Sigewize,
a woman who went preaching,
maddened by devils, or subversive.
She saw the Abbess as harsh ruler,
wrinkled Scrumpilgard,
her rival and her only cure,
the exorcist who knew her mind
and made seven priests with rods
beat the demons of assertion out of her.
Ritual assault for one's own good:
no room for two sibyls at a time.
The devils left, said Hildegard,
with dreadful purging
from the private parts.
Sigewize, broken in,
joined the holy order.

How could she crack the mould
for others, herself chosen
by rare annunciation? Why
should she wish to break
those whirling crystal spheres
within her mind? We measure her
against our models of disorder,
dismantling the world,

but in her songs and sequences
    O vis aeternitatis
even for us, light expands.
Air circles out to the edge of time.

References:

Text: *Opera Omnia* and *Vita* in *Patrologia Latina*, Vol. 197, ed. J-P. Migne, Paris, 1882.
Hildegard of Bingen: An Anthology: ed. F. Bowie, O. Davies, transl. R. Carver, 1990.
P. Dronke, *Women Writers of the Middle Ages*, Cambridge, 1984.
S. Flanagan, *Hildegard of Bingen: A Visionary Life*, London, 1989.

Peter Porter

Since arriving in Britain from his native Australia more than fifty years ago, Peter Porter has published sixteen books of poems, plus four with the Australian painter, Arthur Boyd, and has been the winner of many awards and prizes, including The Queen's Medal for Poetry, and the Forward Prize (2002). His *Collected Poems* were published in 1999, and two years later Trent Books brought out his *Saving From the Wreck: Essays on Poetry*. Since 1998 Peter Porter has been Visiting Professor of Poetry at Nottingham Trent University.

Some of the poems published in *Take Five 05* have appeared in the *Australian Book Review* and *The Times Literary Supplement*.

AT THE BOTANICAL GARDENS, ROME

For Amelia and Martha

Here we come on smart or well-worn soles
To find and carry home the new tadpoles.

Are Roman frogs more bullish than the Brit?
Does childish pleasure soften pain a bit?

The church, with human sins so firmly proffered,
Will make you an almost unrefusable offer –

Ourselves and animals, dependent on the earth,
Are caught in toils of irresistible birth,

With humans sternly judged by how they live –
Do frogs have any trespass to forgive?

So pick them up, these tadpoles, super-gently,
They can't expect a heaven, recompently;

They're here today (you joke they've gone tomorrow),
They offer an apprenticeship of sorrow,

But what's that to the joy of scooping up
A writhing heap of froglets in a cup

And pouring this confusion in a pail
To keep in some unthinking childish gaol?

And here sententiousness comes crowding in –
Christine and I (the adults), and each twin,

The grandchildren, impeccable *gemelli*,
Undaunted by the slimy and the smelly,

Are in these gardens this bright afternoon,
Cerulean skies above us, but dusk soon

To come down like a clicked-at garage door:
(What, we may ask, are frogs' Spring spawnings for

If not to stimulate an appetite
To cherish now what we'll forget tonight

Just as the nomad hamster which escaped
Ended a fur-ball of amorphous shape?)

These ragged gardens stand in Rome for what's
Left of Nature in a land where pots

Are homes to plants, and balconies
Loom *Duce*-like on terra-cotta seas

And TV aerials *per esempio*
Must vie with circus, arch and tempio.

But now back to our sheep (or frogs that is) –
Sheep in mosaic promise Christian *satis*.

Since this has been so far the exposition,
Let's pause before we finish off our mission!

PART TWO

As bristling tadpoles make the water wavery
An urgent noise comes from the *lungotavere*

Where Rome's impatient traffic calls us home
And gaze is turned towards the tallest dome

Of dozens which divide the wide horizon
And spires are hour-hands to help fix eyes on

The works of God they claim to symbolise –
Hang-dog devotion or control's high-rise.

A muddy trudge and now we're at the gates;
A way along the *Farnesina* waits,

Not our direction – our buckets and ourselves
Avoid the gaudy *alimentary* shelves

And head past *Belli's* statue to the steps
Up from the road where Royston, our *Princeps*,

Maintains the KRAMO home, from where you look
At all Rome spread before you like a book.

Nearby, the poet's tophat looks more louche
Than baseball cap worn backwards, more farouche

Than ragged jeans or stripiest hot pants
And just as worthy of an envious glance.

The tadpoles now have made their pilgrimage –
Alas, they'll never grow to full frog stage,

But Marth and Millie grow up by the minute –
O brave new world that has such people in it!

This is the poem's end. Thus Memory,
You reunite us in a place where we

Were happy once and may be so again,
The why and where assured, though not the when.

WHEREOF WE CANNOT SPEAK

There is nothing here 'whereof'. We are
philosophers and drainmakers,
prospectus-holders, vainly gripping
the under-edge of a minor star.

On which we know we can't stay quiet.
How many sonnets must we write
before the great gong sounds in Heaven?
And is this calm a call to riot?

A species which feels sorry for
not just itself, but worms and bats,
would like to make life fair and take
the wrinkles out of sex and war.

Under the microscope it seems
to be covered in odd parasites
called words, and like the pigeon must
talk to walk, nodding at dreams.

Self-lecturing, it fills the Hall
with topoi and parameters
and delegates with names on badges
fulminating where they sprawl.

The brain floats on a lake of words,
just as once the world was held
on elephant-back above a sea –
subversive rhyme suggests that herds

Of metaphors with sharper beak
tear at the silence of unease:
a philosopher feels on his cheek
the tears of which he cannot speak.

THE THIRTY-NINE ARTICLES

> Die Leuchte ha! Die Leuchte verlischt!
>   — *Tristan und Isolde*

And the greatest of these is, "God
    We trust, does not exist."
Anglicans have their own iPod
To download once and future tunes —
Ours a sure footing in the mist,
    And reading of the runes.

Somewhere in the German dark
    A huge complaining mouth
Is siphoning the truth of Bach
Into a death-devoted heart —
The North is blanketing the South
    In saturated art.

Safer than music, words will show
    The temper of the race.
Formal creeds are slow to grow
In English minds: the door's ajar —
Thirty-Nine Steps, and we may trace
    What thing it is we are.

IS THIS A POLITICAL SONNET?
TICK THE APPROPRIATE BOX

☐ NO

although it seeks to write of discontent
With *Astra-Zeneka* and *Vodafone*,
The desert-facing towers of Gabarone,
World-rulers pissing in, not out the tent,
Murdoch untaxed, a Royal's token rent,
Some politician's well-connected loan,
A sexed-up dossier, a No-Fly Zone –
Such stuff is News to charm the Exigent.

☐ YES

since gossip in the Press has always been
In human traffic a sure go-between
Linking resentment and the power to fight,
A sonnet flecked with random satire may
Assume a disjoint harmony of spite
And be Time's Coin Machine – pay and display!

THE JUDGMENT OF CAMBYSES

This must be a page from The Manual
For the Instructing of Humanity,
Showing the improvement of the Social Order
By the avoidance of personal identification
With Suffering, a turning away to private sanity.

It is also specific to its time and place,
The uncorroded detail of vicinity.
These burghers and bystanders are our cousins,
But unlike us are encoded to accept
Adjacence as the only adjunct of Affinity.

The horror has to show itself: a grin
Is the keyboard of Sensation.
Technicians are consulting their circuit-boards –
Knives gripped between their teeth, the torturers
Are unwrapping the skin of Incarnation.

Gerard David, Bruges' Master Painter,
Enters a plea of Authenticity
Making redundant any further Judgment,
And yet, by seeing simply what he sees,
Confronts Intelligence with its complicity.

IMPROVISATION A.M.

At the main point of courage it is never enough
to know that later you will be sure your discretion
is the better part of Valium, and that the offers –

(was that lady truly suggesting that you and she
were likely to be natural sexual partners by reason
of age and shared nationality? Did your meeting with
your champion of years back somehow make up for
the plethora of young writers who are hard pressed
to know who you are, a triple decade on?)

these and such other strangulating moments
wait upon half-awake morning hours, but strangely
a creative indifference warms the bed, and anything
becomes possible, indeed virtuosic – it is only words
and these have been shuffled through as many minds
as leaves which fell last night – some may have belonged
to Coleridge and others to anonymous executioners. The joy
of words without responsibility is not the same
as the irresponsibility of words which have no meaning.

Our lives are swamped by other needs, attempting
impossible explanations in a medium where
they don't apply. Oh, how we wish for diamonds
of exposition, moon-lit as the bath-plunge when *Titanic*
took a century's laughter into unechoing draughts.
One meagre benison remains, as syntax tells us how
the structure of our brains contrives to satisfy
our eyes – in hopeful conversation, "this", we say,
"makes sense", not "is sense", and never just "the case" –

the poet is a laker, a baker and a candlestick maker –
he and she are kneading sense, sprinkling meaning's flour
on their loaves of lines. And to add richness,
puns and serious misunderstandings
light up the sombre ceiling. History flares the path:
an illustrated book explains that London's
Underground could never have been built
without the efforts of the Irish Navy!

UP CLOSE

Our composition of the world as world
is a camera oscura inward-scanning.

One which insists on seeing things up close
so that disasters are too large to fit.

Even indignation adopts a stance,
the gaping dead imprinted on live mouths.

From the latest fire-show on CNN
runs Truth embarrassed by its rebel self

To watch its friends act as epitomes
of what could in no sense be otherwise.

Another wage claim points the way to Gulag,
Inequality the guarantor of Liberty.

This is yourself – you can come in no closer,
God in the mirror sharing Time with you.

Halfway out, and are you dead? Death makes
so little difference to the colour scheme.

Now change the light – say not the struggle naught
et cetera. And Westward what is bright?

Martin Borman's eyes and Bach's enclose
the heritage of all Millennia.

GEORGE CRABBE AT "THE WHITE HART"

Here steppeth out the Old Saltmaster's Son
To unrefine respectability.
He lets them guess he's scheming poetry;
An ounce of living yet may weigh a ton.

At Slaughden he discovered Verse can paint
All Nature is the hues of Paradise –
An inverse Paradise of course, where Vice
Enjoys the pure indifference of a Saint.

He's always been as healthy as a tree –
The sap ascends, the bark is left behind
And sheep-bells tuned in thirds and fifths remind
A tone-deaf poet of Life's poverty.

AT THE REUNION OF THE ANSWERS

They have long forgotten what their questions were
but know their right to be in history.

Some still look fashionably pert,
not perhaps the ones expected to do well.

You meet the cleverest people of your generation,
but who are these who've gathered here today?

Reaching for another glass, a suit pronounces
'For a time I thought the massacre my fault.'

Two uniforms are trading truths. 'War or History,
if one won't fit, the other will.'

One less well-dressed asserts: 'Some who snub me
are living off dividends I bequeathed them.'

A few at the function are hoping to encounter
the reason why they loathed their wives and mothers.

Administrator One remembers how
he drew the border down the middle of a lake.

Administrator Two wears a button-hole
fashioned from a long dismantled pulpit.

As with Archaeology, the temptation
has been to paint the scenes which should be there.

2B or not 2B – how soft a lead
will make truth everlasting?

A fork in the road – The Ass of Buridan
or Pope's provision, 'Whatever is, is right'.

All may anticipate a good death-bed
and, like Miss Stein, set a question to the answer.

RIDING WITH DANTE

Again I find our *cappo dei capi*
A peevish dull provincial, or at best,
Some God-soaked arcane Hammurapi

Intending laws to fit the fitful West
Whose long withdrawal from the edges of
The sun made Medieval minds divest

Themselves of even self-protecting love
To frame instead such torture houses as
Dread and disease below might site above.

These were the rules which said 'Who has
A mind must choose inexorably
Between the Self and Scriptured Caritas.'

It was as though the living Human Tree
Was willing its own rot, and punishment
Were the daylight Dante drew, which he,

Consumed by fear, would go on to present
As God's Rogation – Tuscan automaton,
He knew the azure-sky was Heaven-sent

Like Tuscan cruelty and the Tuscan tongue,
A language for all Italy and soon
A text for scholar-dogs to roll upon.

If Milton's Satan, facing God's harpoon
And cannonade, were silliness enough,
At least the thinking rose above cartoon.

The Inferno's torture-rings are Tolkien stuff,
Grotesques which lack Bosch-like variety,
With everywhere a party-political puff.

Yes, Dante hated well. And, yes, we must agree
His *terza rima* is a Catholic chaconne
Set on a ground as sound as Middle C.

Yet should such unity be insisted on
To please the Great for whom high rank on earth
Is not sufficient boost? Some rare 'haut ton'

It seems was Dante's instinct of Man's worth
Which Pound and Yeats and Eliot took up
To rack their time's indifference to high birth.

'La sua voluntade è mostra pace' – yup!
Thus Ezra's yawp; thus Eliot's feline
Clawing at his Age; thus, too, the Cup

Of Blood, apotheosis of red wine,
A ritual established to redeem
Each human soul that's lived since Constantine.

The problem is this universal dream
Shrouds the momentary and particular
Which then redounds with hot imagined scream

In faction as Imagination's blur
Invents a world where all opponents burn
And God looks on: 'I am, before you were.'

Each system of belief is forced to learn
A dogma and doxology which keeps
The martyr's nerve up facing his *Infern* –

o, the very same in which much later weeps
The heretic of this now puissant Faith –
So Truth's triumphant and Compassion sleeps.

Perhaps I envy each unhappy wraith
Who rises from the turbulence of Hell,
Since in my hands not even rhyme is safe.

For they're immortalised by what they tell
And we who read can guess they're pleased to be
In shit, if there's no other place to dwell.

Alas, it comes down to publicity;
Poets harangue and bully and profess
And feign to publish through eternity.

The dictionary folds them to her breast.

Gregory Woods

Gregory Woods was born in Egypt in 1953. His family having moved to the Gold Coast during the Suez crisis, he spent much of his childhood in the newly independent Ghana. He was educated at a Roman Catholic public school in Oxfordshire and at the University of East Anglia. He began his teaching career at the University of Salerno, erstwhile headquarters of the alchemists, in 1980.

Woods now works at Nottingham Trent University, where he was appointed Professor of Gay and Lesbian Studies in 1998. His was the first such appointment in the United Kingdom. His poetry collections are *We Have the Melon* (1992), *May I Say Nothing* (1998) and *The District Commissioner's Dreams* (2002), all from Carcanet Press. He is also the author of a number of critical books, including *Articulate Flesh: Male Homo-eroticism and Modern Poetry* (1987) and *A History of Gay Literature: The Male Tradition* (1998), both from Yale University Press, and *This Is No Book: A Gay Reader* (1994), from Mushroom Publications.

Acknowledgement:

'Sir Osbert's Complaint' was originally commissioned by the East Midlands Literature Officers Network as part of the *24/8* project supporting the region's writers.

SIR OSBERT'S COMPLAINT

Part One

1

When a thousand coal-gas crocuses ignite like pilot lights
In the grass between the tree trunks, and the scented air excites
Both the senses and the intellect, we long for shorter nights.

2

By the time they've flickered out the air is warmer by degrees
And, depressing though the drizzle is, at least it doesn't freeze.
There's a feeling of renewal on the saturated breeze.

3

Sure enough, the afternoons become reluctant to give way
To the moment when our nanny calls us children in from play
And we dawdle by the door before relinquishing the day.

4

Not that play was what we did when out of sight and out of mind.
If a child had the effrontery to ask us, we declined.
Given books instead of playthings, we were not the playing kind.

5

The society our parents kept we mimicked in our own:
Their jejune, dogmatic arguments; that hyperbolic tone;
And the scenes we'd seen two adults act without a chaperone.

6

But our parodies were arid: we forgot to be amused.
The lampoon and the reality were hopelessly confused.
We became the very adults we'd complacently abused.

Part Two

7

A new century came in. The motorcar replaced the horse.
Every bath we took was heated by the coal mine at its source.
(The industrial's the only revolution I endorse.)

8

Oily rainbows on the fishpond, flaky cinders on the lake,
Claggy slagheaps on the skyline and domestics on the take –
Yet there's nothing in Arcadia that our gardens couldn't fake.

9

At a distance from reality the hedges lead the eye
Into Italy or ancient Greece beneath a leaden sky,
With a fountain or a temple to identify them by.

10

Though our daffodils are hardly more Italian than the Swedes,
Cultivating them is more a deed of habit than Candide's.
What would make it more Italianate would be a clump of weeds.

11

Every vista has a gist, a sort of statement of a creed,
Unbelievable in beauty but in logic guaranteed
To attract one to the factor to which all perspectives lead.

12

Never accurate, the sun-dial is a wiser judge of time
Than the most acute chronometer's mechanic pantomime.
Tempus fugit says enough, obscured by moss and hardened slime.

Part Three

13

Conversational location shaped the content of our talk.
Disagreements were concluded by a choice where footpaths fork,
The direction of our thoughts by the direction of the walk.

14

It was easy to escape whatever choking atmosphere
Was reducing them to silence in the adult stratosphere:
Any path or passageway could make an infant disappear.

15

Mother Nature, as we knew her, had an organising mettle,
Like a nanny. Telling stories to enthral us, she would settle
Our anxieties with posies. We knew nothing of the nettle.

16

I was not so much a bookworm as a bookish sort of leech,
Draining books of every corpuscle of what they had to teach.
(I had heard the mermen singing, in my daydreams, each to each.)

17

I remember with relief a play I wrote while still a child:
Not a word did it contain but what I stole from Oscar Wilde.
It was torn up by my sister, whose good taste it had defiled.

18

Though precocious as a reader, as a writer I was slow.
Masquerading as an author, I mistook the easy flow
Of my nib for wit, parading everything I didn't know.

Part Four

19

With the loyalty a Boyar feels for sullen Mother Russia,
One attempts to save one's ancestry from time's remorseless
  crusher.
What the Sitwells feel for Renishaw, the Ushers felt for Usher.

20

When a home's been in your family this long, you feel related
To each Godforsaken stone. And that's the very thing I hated:
Like my brother it was haunted, like my sister crenellated.

21

It's the typical estate: a country house in formal grounds,
Rambling woods, a lake to boat on, open fields to ride to hounds,
A view beyond to wooded hillsides, the horizon out of bounds.

22

Like the dynasty it serves, rough-hewn by long vicissitude,
Irrespective of the point from which its oddity is viewed,
The aesthetic of the building is by any standard crude.

23

Where you might expect a doorway, there's a brutal chimneystack,
Like a boxer's broken nose on which you dare not turn your back.
Yet the building seems defensive as if tensed for an attack.

24

Horizontal, squat, as grey as Sheffield's weather, this façade
Serves as backdrop to the lives we act out under the regard
Of the statues on the lawn, our audience and bodyguard.

Part Five

25

What with Sachy holding back, and what with Edith holding forth,
With yours truly in the middle, holding little of much worth,
We established all the habits that would mark our time on Earth.

26

We enjoyed ourselves, though sober in the thrust of our hilarity:
For such purpose as we had was to abolish a disparity
By donating Sitwell brilliance to the national culture's charity.

27

Our modernity was earnest. We conducted an impassioned
Celebration of the new – but we preferred our newness rationed.
Though mere novelty wears off, you can rely on the old-fashioned.

28

In the country we conducted our concerns by candlelight
Well into the nineteen-fifties, and kept faith with anthracite.
Reading verse through megaphones would hardly put the past to flight.

29

What we managed as a trio we could not have done apart.
We were thought of as a single beast, a Cerberus of art,
Whose three contrapuntal voices represented just one heart.

30

All for one and one for all! ... I was distracted from this course
By a fourth, one David Horner. Our affair involved, perforce,
Being granted from my siblings an emotional divorce.

Part Six

31

There's a way love has of catching one completely unawares,
As if organised by Providence to herd us into pairs,
With no leisure in our pleasure to make sense of our affairs.

32

We reject discrimination as if throwing off our cares
And commit ourselves to Eros's imaginative snares,
Too enchanted by a hairstyle to have time for splitting hairs.

33

It's a platitude: the smaller things are bigger than the bigger.
I met David. He seemed civilised, and vigorous in figure.
If romance requires an instrument, his silk tie was its trigger.

34

I was always the pursuer, he was always the pursued.
Like a virgin pleading modesty, he forged my servitude
With reluctance so convincing I was utterly subdued.

35

In the manner of the ancients, he became my other half.
Though it might have been expected that we'd kill the fatted calf,
We discreetly shared a bottle, a bread pudding and a laugh.

36

Being often seen together, we were treated as a pair.
No one asked the question no one answered: colleague, friend, affair?
In the end, we dared to share a *pied-à-terre* in Carlyle Square.

Part Seven

37

If one quails at being crushed beneath an omnibus, or coshed,
In their denser concentrations one avoids the great unwashed.
From a height they look like insects. How one prays they could be
    squashed!

38

With society sclerotic and the culture half asleep,
Nothing changes for the better, nothing moves but at a creep.
It would take a leopard shepherd to direct this herd of sheep.

39

Mussolini had the right idea to save a nation's pride.
I had hopes that Oswald Mosley could, colossus-like, bestride
What was left of Merrie England, but my optimism died.

40

When the blackshirts came to Renishaw they started with a march
From their charabancs along the drive and through the gothic arch,
But the stiffness of their uniforms proved little more than starch.

41

We retreated to the house for the duration of the war,
But despite the country setting we weren't spared the bombers'
    roar.
They were aiming at poor Sheffield, but just missing Renishaw.

42

What kept us there together, more the bloodline than the heart,
Was fidelity to family and passion for our art –
Plus the fact we had our rooms a hundred yards or so apart.

Part Eight

43

In the orchard, Edith overcomes the words with which she grapples
And records her peerless triumph on the page the sunlight dapples.
If the worse comes to the worst, the shadows comfort her with
  apples.

44

When it comes to deeds of derring-do, some talk of Alexander.
But Hephaestion is left till adulation turns to slander.
I remember both when David is demobbed, a Wing Commander.

45

The returning hero hurries to discard his uniform,
Like Odysseus in the bedroom in the calm after the storm,
All the more the welcome husband for his relapse to the norm.

46

These two people I love most seem never quite on speaking terms:
To discuss the weather with them is to stir a can of worms,
And mere greetings pass between them like a frank exchange of
  germs.

47

Rhododendron bushes guard the English like defensive banks,
As intimidating as the sand dunes hiding Rommel's tanks,
But they flower in an hour like a fusillade of blanks.

48

In a deckchair on the terrace in the sunshine, David dozes.
When you try to think, your mind goes pink with the scent of
  bloated roses.
What mankind proposes, God ignores, and matter decomposes.

Part Nine

49
Unexpectedly one sees one's seen the last of the wisteria.
From now on the shadows lengthen and the flowerbeds are
    drearier.
The high season is succeeded by its lachrymose inferior.

50
Irretrievable, time passes. Things get worse. The waistline thickens.
Was it God who made us kneel to *hoi polloi*, or was it Dickens?
Clement Attlee did the dirty work whose legacy still sickens.

51
In their element, all metals tarnish, oxidize or rust.
Carpe diem, if you must, but don't blame me if uncurbed lust
Leaves you feeling life's worth living, an illusion you can't trust.

52
Waking early, I can hear the garden boy is raking leaves.
I can picture how his muscles play below his rolled-up sleeves.
No physique was better fitted to light gardening since Eve's.

53
Though he's bulky as a boxer, his self-consciousness is louche,
And his sulkiness is lovable, less thuggish than farouche.
How unmissable to kiss his – what's the word for it? – his *bouche*!

54
If I dress and hurry down I'll find no Corydon, but just
Dead leaves scudding through the doorway on a cold, autumnal
    gust.
Golden lads and girls all must, like carpet-sweepers, come to dust.

Part Ten

55

If the levellers had time while they reduced the Welfare State
To its lowest common multiple, they might anticipate
What the absence of the beautiful would leave us with, but hate.

56

They prefer one to have castles in not Italy but Spain,
Built with fantasies and figments, like a segment of Cockaigne,
So that nobody should benefit from beauty's rich demesne.

57

What has art to do with anything, or anything that matters,
If, instead of hitching beauty to the truth, it merely flatters
Ideologies – an enema for dormice and mad hatters?

58

One's life follows its own sequence, like a living alphabet,
In which brandy follows port, a hacking cough a cigarette,
Spelling out its narrative, and never sidetracked or upset.

59

When a writer's philosophical – I am, therefore I think –
He distends his cogitations with incontinence of ink,
As if nothing could suppress him but a bullet or a shrink.

60

Freud has probably identified some syndrome of the pen,
A neurosis in which childhood reasserts its hold on men.
Diagnosis is straightforward, but the cure beyond our ken.

Part Eleven

61
Since a night when I was sleepless and some presence slapped my
    cheek
I've been reconciled to dying. The revenges they might wreak
Keep the spirits fit and active in their games of hide and seek.

62
Planning hauntings of his enemies beguiles an old man's time:
I shall lurk behind the arras like a witness to some crime,
Taunting Philistines and critics in the fashion of my prime.

63
When I'm dead I'll have no deadline but untold eternities.
Without feet I'll creak the floorboards, without hands I'll jangle
    keys.
When I go is up to God, if not to Parkinson's disease.

64
The old sawmill by the lake looks like a grounded man o' war
In the helicopter flicker of the shedding sycamore
While I wander, humming Walton, through the woods at
    Renishaw.

65
As a boy I gathered conkers here and carried them indoors,
Looking after them as if they were the eggs of chests of drawers.
I imagined I could hatch antiques to rival Renishaw's.

66
Like the hero of the epic, I found trouble at my door.
I'd come home for some repose, but quoth the haven: Nevermore.
There were more than ghosts to haunt me in the halls of Renishaw.

Part Twelve

67
Could that tapping of a finger on the glass be Peter Quint,
Or an agitated, leafless branch delivering a hint
Of the Reaper's urgency, enough to crack a heart of flint?

68
Could that rustle in the passage, like a paper carnivore,
Or like a present being wrapped, be someone wrapping at my door?
Could I be becoming nervous of the sounds of Renishaw?

69
Could that tapping at the window or the rustle in the corner
Be material expressions, from the living building's fauna,
Of unease – the moths and dormice, getting bored with David Horner?

70
There are times when love is war, however long the corridor.
I had nowhere to escape to. When you're cloistered with a bore
Life's a prison. Nowhere's big enough, not even Renishaw.

71
Make the most of what you've got. The rest's for God to reimburse.
One could do a great deal worse to mitigate old age's curse
Than attach oneself to someone who can double as a nurse.

72
Love's no less a form of ownership with equal than with chattel.
I employed a man my most abusive tantrums failed to rattle.
The result was a romance with which I fought a losing battle.

Part Thirteen

73

What did David's love amount to but a relic from the past?
As ephemeral as summer, it was never meant to last.
It's enough that we had years together nothing else surpassed.

74

When I've pointed out some trinket in the hope he'll be impressed,
I've been comforted to hold him at a distance, yet distressed
To discover that my lover is now just another guest.

75

If I see him in the bathroom, greying hairs on flabby chest,
I dissociate him from the golden boy I once caressed;
I can hardly recognise this stranger, shaving in his vest.

76

Once, his absences upset me; now, his presence just depressed.
The solution was for him to leave. ('It might be for the best.')
Let him sacrifice himself: for *dulce et decorum est*.

77

It was now I chose to choose between the past and future tenses
By exchanging David Horner for my new amanuensis
And, in some eyes, taking leave of both my homeland and my senses.

78

Since I shied away from telling him myself, I went one better
And instructed my solicitor to do it in a letter:
Sir, my client is dismissing you as his onlie begetter.

Part Fourteen

79

I'm tempted to pre-empt the dusk. The indoor status quo
Is asserted with drawn curtains, blocking out the heavens' glow.
Either Sheffield's lit its streetlights or it's coming on to snow.

80

By the dawn the middle lawn is like a bridal featherbed.
On the yews we use to limit it, a dimity's been spread,
Like a dust-sheet over furniture when everyone has fled.

81

Nothing stains the linen's virtue but the footprints of a fox
And the silence makes it whiter like the stopping of the clocks
Or the vague, intrusive presence of an absent chatterbox.

82

But by nightfall it's been sleeting and the snow's begun to melt,
The bridal bed's been covered with a blanket of grey felt.
Not that spring is yet upon us; but one wintry spell is spelt.

83

If the breeze is from the east you can make out the M1's cars,
For the isle is full of noises, and the slightest zephyr mars
What it ventilates. The very welkin tarnishes the stars.

84

The austerity of breeding is a burden I've passed on
To my brother, whom posterity relies on for a son.
Where the first-born yields, the second has a first-born of his own.

85

As my father did before me, I'd decided to withdraw
To a warmer garden's scenery on terraces galore.
To the English, I left England; to my nephew, Renishaw.

Part Fifteen

86

Give me peace and beauty, peace and beauty, silence with a view;
And a man without opinions to explain the beauty to.
Or, failing that, there's Proust: *À la recherche du temps perdu.*

87

If the Muses had allowed me to alleviate the pain
Of nostalgic longing for a time I'd rather not regain,
I might have said: Last night I dreamt I went to Renishaw again.

88

But, in truth, I've had my fill of it, as it has had of me.
It takes more than bricks and mortar to support a threnody.
If I dream of anything, these days, it's of mortality.

89

I was not the kind of man who always wondered what things meant.
It sufficed that they existed for me, whether Heaven-sent
Or the product of Contingency, that dapper malcontent.

90

I keep asking my own conscience if I ever used my eyes
To do more than seek one falsehood in a lethal pack of lies,
Seeing nothing of the truth throughout a life of compromise.

91

I imagine I've a badge in one of Heaven's pending trays,
Saying, Sceptical believer with a decent turn of phrase.
That's the best that I can hope for when the last trump duly plays.

92

What endures? A thousand pages of my memoirs. Little more.
Edith's poems, at a pinch. And Sachy's offspring. Little more.
And the Sitwell seat at Renishaw. There's this and little more.